PUT AWAY
CHILDISH THINGS

DR. KIRK LEWIS

PRESS

DEDICATION

I grew up in the small,
Texas Panhandle farming community of Ropesville.
In deference to Garrison Keillor,
a much drier and dust-blown
Lake Wobegon.

Two individuals stand out among those
hard-working, "above average" residents of my hometown.
Gene and Earline Lewis,
my parents.

Endowed with
common sense and innate intelligence.
Compassionate and caring.
They practiced a "pull the ox out of the ditch" kind of Christianity.
Concerned more about serving than self...
more about righteousness than ritual.

You could find the most appealing character traits
demonstrated by the men and women in this book
exhibited in the lives of my parents.
Mom passed away in 1998,
but Dad continues to live life to the fullest,
in obedience to his God and
in service to his neighbors.

They shaped my soul.

Because of the testimony of their lives,
I dedicate this book to two of my favorite people.

ACKNOWLEDGEMENTS

Barnabas.
The Encourager.

The Apostle Paul thanked God for the encouragement he received
from his friend and fellow minister, Barnabas.
I suspect in the hardest times of Paul's life he remembered
Barnabas' arm around his shoulder...
a silly joke to break the tension...
a soft, reassuring word whispered in his ear...
a slight nod from the back of the crowd,
letting the evangelist know his sermon was right on target.

As I began this process,
I found my Barnabas looked a lot like my wife, Robin.
She believed more strongly in my ability
to tell a story than I believed myself.
Thank you, Robin,
for the genuine encouragement and unfailing love.

I give my appreciation and love
for the support of my sons and daughters-in-law...
Adam and Jordan,
parents to my precious grandchildren,
Eli and Josiah.
Andrew and Melissa
(parents of any future grandchildren born into this union).

They inspired my writing.

Special gratitude to others who reinforced my efforts:

Dr. Ron Lyles, my pastor…

Leslie Lewis, my uncle…

Diana de los Santos, the first person to encourage my writing,

Joan Neal, a friend…

Candace Ahlfinger and Sherry Bufkin,

colleagues and friends…

Thank you to a host of family, friends and neighbors

who read the occasional chapter

or lifted me up in prayer.

You have blessed my life.

TABLE OF CONTENTS

Put Away Childish Things

Bible stories for children,
by their nature,
carry simple messages.
As a child,
I heard them all.
I got the message.

"God loves me."
"God calls me."
"God guides me."
"God protects me."
"God provides for me."

Those same stories taught me that
in response to His love and provision…

"God desires my faith."
"God requires my obedience."
"God deserves my trust."

Simple messages.
Simple truths.
Simple times.
For that time in my life,
simple was sufficient.

I carved the features of some of these biblical heroes
on my spiritual Mt. Rushmore.

Noah.
Abraham.
David.
Daniel.

For others, I erected smaller statues,
posed on ornate pedestals in the recesses of my mind,
bronzed plaques extolling their virtues.

Isaac.
Miriam.
Gideon.
Ruth.
Jonah.

I imagined them...
Impeccably dressed in brightly-colored,
neatly-pressed robes.
Shoulders back.
Heads high.
Knees calloused
from supplication and prayer.
Men and women who walked with God.

They spoke in King James English.
Sang "Holy, Holy, Holy"
in perfect pitch and pulsating vibrato.
Deep and serious intent in their hearts.
Men who righted every wrong.
Virtuous women.
Unblemished personal character.
Finest moral fiber.
Deepest devotion.
Passionate.
Pious.
Perfect.

God can use people like that, I reasoned.
God can use people
who never waver in faith.
Who never doubt God's strength and purpose.
Who never fail to allow God to use them
in a miraculous way to accomplish His will and way.
Whose extraordinary devotion and exceptional deed
serve as unimpeachable examples of Godly living.

God can use people like that,
but God has little use for

someone

like

me.

Imperfect. Impulsive.
Selfish. Stubborn.
Simple message.
Simple truth.
Simply short-sighted.

*

With age,
childhood lessons learned at the feet of parents
disappeared in the fog of daily living.
My "Mt. Rushmore" cracked.
My statues tumbled from their pedestals,
covered in dust and buried in the brambles.
My Bible heroes weathered.
Unrecognizable.
Unwanted.
Unreal.

Little more than two-dimensional caricatures
stuck to a flannel board,
relegated in memory to the
isolated corner of a darkened Sunday School classroom
in a small, rural church.

With age,
the stories seemed shallow.
A colorless landscape.
Devoid of emotion.
Expressionless.
Exhausted.

They were…
Too pure.
Too perfect.

Therefore, less alluring.
Less applicable.
Less relevant.
Less.

"Build a boat, Noah."
Noah stubbornly built a boat.
No questions.
No self-consciousness.
No sense of the grave responsibility he carried.

"Sacrifice your son, Abraham."

Abraham blindly obeyed.

No confusion.

No anger.

No sense of the example of redemption God called him to be.

"Slay the giant, David."

David fearlessly found a stone.

No queasy stomach.

No trepidation.

No hesitation.

No sense of the very real danger he faced.

"Pray only to God, Daniel."

Daniel steadfastly bowed his head.

No defiance.

No finger-pointing.

No sense of exasperation in the face of the evil men do.

Then, I discovered

God's method in the inspired madness of Scripture.

Leave the story vague.

Let me fill in the blanks

germane to my world...

my time...

my life.

Let me learn to live as God desires me to live
by seeing the world through the
eyes and experiences of
extraordinary,
ordinary
men and women of faith.

Less
became
More.

More personal.
More passionate.
More perfect.

More of what I needed to find truth in God's Word.
Truth to guide.
Truth to teach.
Truth to live.
Truth that surpasses understanding.

When I was a child, I talked like a child,
I thought like a child,
I reasoned like a child.
When I became a man,
I put away childish things.
—I Corinthians 13:11

HOW BAD COULD IT BE?

Genesis 6:9-8:22

How bad could it be?

With the snap of a divine finger,
the Creator of the world created an explosion whose reverberations
still echo through the universe for time upon time.

The beginning.

Matter spinning against matter,
expanding through the void,
leaving it dotted with chunks of rock and gas
boiling in some primordial mixture of inspired design.
To Light and Darkness He gave each its own place.

His consciousness settled on one particular mass,
the third indistinct rock from an insignificant sun,
one among billions.
Dragging his finger lightly across the landscape,
He carved the mountains and scooped out the oceans.
Set it spinning through space in perfect lockstep with the universe.
Everything within His created realm
functioned in clocklike precision.

Created it all.

It was good. It was very good.

But, the best was yet to come.

Sculpting the red clay into a distinctive form,
God's breath fluttered across the face
made of a glob of dust and mud.
Life came to His most intimate creation.
Man walked in a distant garden,
connected to the Creator in
thought,
heart
and soul.

Too lonesome...Too alone.
This would never do.
A deep sleep...A shared rib.
A delightful difference.

Two became One.
Man and Woman,
mirrored image of the
Master Biologist.

Loving...
Compassionate...
Free.

It was good. It was very good.

But the worst was yet to come.

*

One bad choice derailed perfection.
One stray thought.
One arrogant expression.
One disobedient act
spun the world out of control.
Goodness lost its hold on the heart.

Those responsible for disobedience
fled from the
face of the Father
who walked among them.
Naked souls laid bare by selfishness.
Hearts turned away by rebellion.
Innocence lost by personal choice.

Expelled from Eden,
but not abandoned or alone,
for the Creator God walked with them.
Never more than a prayer away.

A distance that proved too far.

*

Disobedience begat disobedience.
Every decadent thought in the mind of man
collided and conjoined
like two beads of mercury on the tabletop.
Each new perversion larger than the last.

How bad could it be?

Murder and Madness.
Selfishness and Sin.
Larceny and Lust.
Wickedness and Wantonness.
Cruelty and Capriciousness.

Bad beyond belief!

The Creator mourned for His Creation.
Perfection soiled.
Relationship strained.
Deepest regret settled in the depths of His heart.
Resignation followed.

Forgiving eyes, filled with tears, fell on the righteous remnant.
God's hope resonated in the faithful hearts of one man and
his family.

"And Noah found grace in the eyes of the Lord."

The Creator God walked with Noah and
Noah walked with God.
Their daily talks filled with longing for better.
Noah, in deep conversation with God,
heard serious implications for the world.

An assured destruction.
A blueprint for salvation.

Cubits, by cubits, by cubits.
A little cypress wood. A lot of pitch.
A collection of all living things.

And the righteous man did all God commanded.

The earth shook and the thunder rolled,
the sound of God's fury focused on a selfish world
teeming with ungodly intentions.
Heaven's floodgates opened.
The deep springs broke forth.
Torrential rains fell.
Waters swallowed the face of the earth.

Forty days and forty nights.
God destroyed it all.
The waters rose and washed away all evil.
A cleansing flood.

What can wash away all sin?
Nothing but the flood.

The ark and its faithful few floated freely upon the waves
until the waters of the flood receded,
revealing a new world glistening with hope.
Brimming with promise.

An all-powerful, all-knowing God offered a fresh start.
A chance to set the world on a righteous path.
A covenant extended by a loving God.

A rainbow in remembrance of the provision of grace
offered by a loving God to a people
whose *every inclination of the heart was toward evil from birth
unto death.*

Grace

The faith demonstrated by Noah and his family was not a per-
fect faith.
Nor were they simply righteous by comparison
to the ungodly world around them.
What set them apart from their neighbors who suffered
God's wrath?
Sin is sin, after all.

Their righteousness acknowledge God as
Creator.
Provider.
Sustainer.
Lord.

Sin led to humble sacrifice and sincere worship.
Disobedience sought the Father's forgiveness.
Flawed gave way to forgiven.

Ultimately,
that flawed faith and countless acts of obedience
drew God's attention.

Selected for a boat ride of a lifetime
God offered Noah a gift he could scarcely fathom.

God asked Noah, "Accept this fantastic tale,"
but also "Act on simple faith
in full view of a world
that would react with ridicule and derision."

Think about that.

Obedience in the face of absurdity.
Submission in the face of scorn.

There was Noah, living in an arid world,
building a boat.
Not just a little fishing boat,
but a cargo ship…
400 feet long…
five stories tall!

Imagine the insecurity and self-doubt.
Noah,
a righteous man of faith,
obeyed.

Storms will come.
Life's waters will rise.
Caused by a lost and troubled world.
Or swirling in the chaos of our own rebellion.

Through it all,
God looks for faith no greater than a mustard seed.
When He finds it,
He extends His grace to the
flawed, yet faithful.

He says, "Build it."
We must build.
He says, "Ride out the storm in the provision of my grace."
We ride it out.

In faith, we obey.
In faith, we start again.

As people in need of saving
time and time again,
God finds a way.
Unmerited favor.
Grace.

For Noah…
a boat of cypress wood.
For us…
a wooden cross and an empty tomb.

A spiritual ark.
A new promise.
A new covenant.

He offered His grace to a sinful world
through Noah,
a farmer turned carpenter.
He offered His grace to our lost world
through Jesus,
a carpenter turned Savior.

All God asks of us in return is faith and obedience in full view
of a suspicious and disobedient world.
For by grace we are saved yesterday, today and tomorrow.

What can wash away my sin?
Nothing but the blood.

For it is by grace you have been saved,
through faith—and this not from yourselves,
it is the gift of God.
—Ephesians 2:8

No Other Way

Genesis 22

The burnt orange clouds reflected the first light of day.
The morning sun added brilliance to the green grass in the valley
and vivid shade of blue to the nearby pond.
Abraham walked quietly to the top of the hill
overlooking the rocky enclosures that corralled his livestock.
A few servants offered feed to the cattle while others milked
the goats.
As he often did,
Abraham reflected on God's manifold gifts.
God's fulfilled promises.
Abraham felt blessed in every way.

In that quiet moment of reflection,
Abraham offered a heartfelt prayer of gratitude
to the One True God whom he had followed obediently
since the days of his spiritual awakening in the land of Haran.

Always receptive to God's call,
Abraham heard a familiar voice in his heart.
The same voice that called him from his father's land.
The same voice that told him to settle in Canaan.
The same voice that said his descendants
would outnumber the grains of sand.
The same voice that told him
he would have a son long after he had reason to hope.
A voice he trusted explicitly.

God called,
"Abraham!"
"Here I am," answered the nomad.

"Take your son."
"Which one?" thought Abraham.
"Ishmael or Isaac?"

God said,
"Your only son."
"I don't understand," wondered Abraham.
"There is no 'only'."

God said,
"The one you love."
"Ah, Isaac," realized Abraham with a gleam in his eye.
God's miraculous gift in his old age.

God said,

"Take him to Moriah."

"An odd request," thought Abraham.

"Why must we go so far north?"

God said,

"Sacrifice him as a burnt offering."

Then, the Voice went Silent.

Abraham staggered.

Stunned.

Shocked.

Speechless.

A voice he trusted asking the unthinkable.

All the color drained from his world.

No orange sun. No green grass. No blue water.

Bleak.

Barren.

Bitter.

"Sacrifice him as a burnt offering."

No amount of faith prepared him for that command.

"Pick up your family. Go to a land I will show you."

Abraham obeyed.

"Settle here in the land of Canaan."

Abraham obeyed.

"Build an altar and worship."
Abraham always obeyed.

"Kill your beloved child."
How could any father obey that directive?

Keeping the still, quiet, disturbing conversation to himself,
Abraham walked as a man condemned.

All day long,
Abraham agonized within his heart.
All day long,
he called for God to explain.
All day long,
all he heard was the inner conflict of his soul.

Lying in his tent late into the evening,
he begged for clarity.
Lying in his tent, still awake in the early morning,
he fought with his soul.
Early in the morning,
Abraham obeyed.
Abraham always obeyed.

Quietly slipping from his tent,
careful to avoid waking Sarah, his wife.
Abraham entered Isaac's tent, shook him awake.
With two servants and a donkey loaded with wood,
Abraham set out on a mindless journey of unsettled obedience.

Abraham walked on autopilot for three days.

A broken man going through the motions.

He refused to speak again to God.

Lost in his twisted hell,

spoke only to answer basic questions.

Journey of three days.

Jagged nerves.

Jumbled thoughts.

How could it be?

His God, his Protector,

his God, his Promise Keeper,

his God, his Partner,

violated the covenant He made.

Required obedience at the cost of life...

Not his own (that he would gladly give)...

but that of his beloved son.

The one who brought laughter to a humorless household.

God's ultimate betrayal.

Abraham camped at the base of Mt. Moriah,

A rocky outcrop covered in stunted brush.

Steeling his nerves,

Abraham looked to the heavens.

God promised Isaac would be the beginning

of an eternal and everlasting family.

If He promised,

Abraham must believe.

Abraham turned to his servants
telling them to remain behind.
"We will go up," said Abraham.
"We will return."

Without understanding fully,
Abraham trusted the only acceptable outcome.
Packing the wood on Isaac's broad shoulders,
and carrying the torch and knife himself,
the father trudged up the mountain with his beloved son.

Absent of reason,
Abraham responded with
firm faith, fixing his eyes on the summit.

*

Isaac.
Object of his father's devotion and love.
For almost 30 years,
he had sat at his father's feet.
Worked side by side.
Talked in private conversations.
Listened and learned.
Grown in deep faith and understanding of
his father's God.
His God.

An odd journey.

Like no other in his life.

Something troubled his father.

The normal light-hearted, continuous banter

between father and son

grew stilted and silent.

Every question elicited a grunt and grimace.

Isaac's attempts at humor…

greeted with silence and a stare.

Isaac respected his father too much

to push for an explanation.

The climb up the mountain seemed to take a toll on his father,

every step a laborious effort.

Isaac worried.

All the provisions of sacrifice

but no lamb.

Curiosity broke the silence at last.

"Father," asked Isaac quietly.

"Where is the lamb?"

The very question Abraham dreaded.

Abraham looked away for a moment.

When he turned to face his son

his eyes filled with tears.

A whisper and a wish,

"God will provide."

A darker cloud settled in Isaac's heart.
Each beat a little faster.
Every breath a little shorter.
Something definitely wrong.

Abraham stooped to pick up two stones.
Together, father and son built an altar.
Isaac noticed each stone his father placed upon the pile glistened
with his tears.
Finally, Isaac piled the wood on the altar,
turning to his father with a questioning look.

"What now?"

*

Tears flowed freely.
Unashamed.
Abraham, beside himself with grief,
hugged his son tightly to his chest.
After a long moment,
he pushed Isaac to arm's length.
With a weak and trembling voice,
Abraham shared the horror that God required.

Three days of inner struggle
convinced Abraham of God's faithfulness.
What God promised, He delivered.
Each time.
Every time.
If God promised a long line of descendants through Isaac,
God would make it so.
Trusting in a God who asked the unfathomable,
Abraham asked Isaac to trust him
and to trust his God.

Isaac searched his father's eyes
for any sign of insanity.
He saw only a father he adored,
a father whose faith had never failed,
a father in whom he believed,
asking him to trust a God in whom he believed.

Isaac could have overpowered his elderly father.
He could have fled and never looked back,
but, in time,
in an act of absolute submission,
Isaac held out his wrists to be bound together.

Abraham wrapped the leather straps around his son's wrists,
whispered prayers on his lips,
tied tightly together the hands he had held as a child.
With a kiss on his father's cheek,
Isaac laid himself on the altar,
a willing and obedient sacrifice.

Abraham recited the identical prayer
he had offered every time a lamb was slain...
A prayer seeking forgiveness and atonement...
A prayer of adoration and worship.

Abraham raised the knife above his head
to slay his beloved son.

"Abraham! Abraham!"
the Voice called to him.
"Here I am," choked Abraham.

The same Voice that called for sacrifice
now offered reprieve.
Nothing withheld by Abraham.
Everything restored by the Father.

A ram, caught in the thicket,
substituted for Isaac upon the altar.
Together father and son worshipped
in full knowledge that
God provided the lamb.

A promise reaffirmed.

Abraham's blessing reaffirmed.

Obedience

"Blind faith."

"Unquestioning obedience."

"Absolute trust."

Little more than pious platitudes

unless tested in the crucible of conviction.

When God whispered Abraham's name in Haran,

the shepherd left his ties behind and journeyed to a distant land.

When the Voice grew silent,

he stopped in his tracks and waited upon the Lord.

When the Voice called again, he moved again.

When the Voice called, he acted....every time.

He obediently placed his life in God's hands.

He endured childlessness until God provided his legacy

in the form of a son,

born to parents long past childbearing years.

Through every twist and turn,

Abraham responded obediently to the Voice in his heart,

fully aware of the blessed life he lived.

Blessings flowed.
God had no right, yet He had every right,
to redeem the gift He had given to Abraham and Sarah.
When He called in the debt,
the cost of faithfulness was astronomical.

God said,
"Kill the son you love.
Offer him as a sacrifice in My Name."
We sit in the comfort of our century
wondering how God could ask such a thing of anyone,
astonished that Abraham could consider such a thing.

Trying to make sense of senselessness, we reason…
Maybe Abraham loved Isaac too much,
placing family above God.
Maybe his worship of God took second place
to his love for his son.
Maybe he became enamored with the idea of Isaac,
as the one through whom Abraham's descendants
would become a mighty nation…God's people.
Heady stuff for a simple nomad.
Maybe God had to teach Abraham a lesson in humility
by claiming what he loved most in this world.

We long to justify God's actions.
Such explanations fail to look deeply enough into
God's character and heart.
The One who made the promise to the shepherd of Haran
never intended Abraham to sacrifice Isaac.
To do so would contradict God's nature and
thwart the commandments He one day set in stone.

To allow us to grasp the unfathomable,
God acted out a play.
A visual testimony to the extreme to which
God would go to redeem a fallen world.
His love deep enough to compel the Creator of all things
to offer His own Son as a sacrifice...
for our sins.

Abraham could have refused,
could have walked away.
In a mind-bending act of trust,
in the face of enormous doubt in his heart,
Abraham complied.
Only in this purposeful and deliberate act of obedience
would we even minutely understand
the gift God offered us through His Son.
If Abraham was a knowing partner in God's intent,
an actor who knew in advance the climax of the story,
it would require no faith.
The offer of sacrifice meaningless.

What God asked of Abraham,
God was willing to do Himself.
He placed His beloved Son on a wooden cross.

Though mystifying by human standards,
Abraham's obedience rises as a metaphor
of the complete and voluntary sacrifice
that God would one day employ.

For the first time in human history,
God tipped His hand in answer
to mankind's betrayal…
a new path to an eternal Eden.

There was no other way for God to
reclaim His creation.
No other way.

"For God so loved the world,
that He gave His only Son,
that whosoever believes in Him should not perish,
but have everlasting life."
—John 3:16

*

(Abraham's name is synonymous with faith and obedience,
Yet there was another actor in God's play whose response
to circumstances provides the rest of the story.
His name is Isaac.)

COMPLETE SURRENDER

Genesis 22

Standing on the dusty mountain,
Isaac looked around as his father stood
quietly and reverently nearby.
All the provisions of sacrifice
but no lamb.
Curiosity broke the silence.

*

"Father," asked Isaac quietly.
"Where is the lamb?"
The very question Abraham
had been dreading for days.
Abraham looked away for a moment.
When he turned to face his son
his eyes filled with tears.
A whisper and a wish,
"God will provide."

A darker cloud settled in Isaac's heart.
Each beat a little faster.
Every breath a little shorter.
Something definitely wrong.

Isaac watched as Abraham stooped to pick up one stone
after another,
Stacking them carefully, forming the foundation of an altar.
Bewildered and bothered,
the son joined in the construction.
Isaac noticed each stone his father placed glistened with his tears.
Finally, with the altar completed,
Isaac piled the wood he had carried and placed it atop the stone
structure.
He turned to his father with a questioning look
as if to say,

"What now?"

*

After moments of silence during which Isaac
heard only the whisper of the wind,
Abraham spoke, his voice weak and raspy.
Isaac heard the words of his father,
spoken in a dull monotone as the tears flowed freely,
each fragment of the story spilling out in gasps between his
heavy sobs.
Isaac listened in macabre fascination and a growing sense of fear.
The Voice he heard of all his life
had again gave new instructions to his father.
Instead of moving to a new land
or entering into a treaty with a neighboring king,
the Voice demanded human sacrifice.

Not just any human.
Isaac himself would substitute for the lamb.

Disbelief.
Bewilderment.
Disorientation.

A flood of emotion.
A deluge of denial.
A surge of anger.
An upwelling of bile in his throat.

Isaac roughly pushed his father away,
searching his eyes for any sign that his
aging father had lost his mind.
He saw none.
Only resigned sadness.
He saw a man whose deep faith
allowed no options.
No other way.

Isaac turned and walked away.
Abraham let him go, dropping to his knees,
his inner turmoil too much to bear.
The young man needed time.
Isaac walked to the edge of a cliff,
staring into the valley below.
The full gamut of emotion raged through his mind.

He had never questioned his father's love…
until now.
The same man who kissed him as a child
now planned to drive a knife into his heart.
The same man who bandaged cuts as a young boy,
the same man who taught him the ways of the land as a teenager,
the same man who shared with him
a divine covenant with the Almighty
that his family would be the beginning of a chosen people,
condemned Isaac to an altar.

Isaac struggled to comprehend.
Why would God change his mind about my future,
a future He ordained?
What heinous sin did I commit
that requires my sacrifice?

Then it occurred to Isaac…
God always demanded the best lamb.
Spotless.
Without blemish.
Am I my father's best offering?

Isaac looked back at his father,
who sat rocking back and forth, knees pulled tightly to his chest,
murmuring soft prayers to God,
the long knife still brandished in his hand.
He couldn't bear the agony he saw in Abraham's eyes,
the internal war written on his face.

What conversation must have passed between father and son?

"Why, father? Why?"
asked Isaac.

Abraham looked into the face of the young man
he raised and cherished since birth.
"I trust God's promises," he said quietly.
"Every promise He made throughout my life,
He kept.
You, my son, stand as proof of His miraculous faithfulness.
God's gift to your mother and me.
So late in life.
He promised descendants through you,
your children and your children's children.
He promised!

"Because He has always been faithful,
I believe He will provide a way to bring life from death.
He will provide a substitute or he will bring you back to me
Somehow,
some way,
some day."

With confidence and conviction,
Abraham looked into his son's eyes and said simply,
"I trust."

*

Isaac walked away again.

Lost in his thoughts.

Lost in his father's words.

In the end, Isaac knew he could run.

His father was in no physical condition to stop him.

Yet, something kept his feet firmly planted.

He never knew his father to act irrationally.

He trusted his father without question.

Trusted his father's trust in God.

Had even learned to trust in God himself.

Isaac took a deep breath,

knelt by his father's side,

gently raised him to his feet,

looked silently into his brown eyes.

The love between Abraham and Isaac evident in their embrace.

The young man surrendered himself to the Father's will.

In an act of absolute submission,

Isaac held out his hands to be bound.

"The Lord will provide."

Father and son prayed those words almost as a mantra

as the leather straps were wrapped around Isaac's wrists.

"The Lord will provide."

In the gravity of that moment,
Isaac, the devoted son,
laid himself upon the altar,
prepared to die.
"The Lord will provide."

No words left to say.
Isaac could have changed his mind,
begged and pleaded for his life.
He could have screamed for mercy.
He could have cursed his father and his God.
He could have bolted beyond his father's reach.
Instead, Isaac prayed a quiet prayer,
"Father, if there is any other way…"
A young man, desiring life,
but willing to die.

As his father raised the knife above his head
Abraham's beloved son closed his eyes.
Isaac heard the Voice calling his father's name.
God's last minute reprieve.
A substitute in the thorns.
A sacrifice of thanksgiving.

A father's act of sacrifice.
A son's act of submission.
God's prophetic pronouncement of profound intent.

Submission

We quickly praise Abraham for his faithfulness.
And he was faithful.
We honor Abraham for his obedience,
even in the face of God's bizarre command.
And he was obedient.
Obedient when most of us would turn away.

But, remember...
Abraham heard the Voice.
Had four days to think it through,
four restless nights to decide his course of action.
He lived a long life intimately aware
of the One who directed his every step...
One who proved himself faithful time and time again.
Contemplation led to compliance.
His past experiences with God compelled his obedience.
Abraham heard the Voice.

Now, consider...
Isaac heard nothing.
No Voice.
No verbal command.

Isaac had no vision.
No days to reflect.
No nights to meditate.
No meaningful past experiences of his own
with the One who guided his steps.

51

No basis for deep-seated trust in the God of his father.

Isaac had mere moments of madness
on an arid mountain in the middle of nowhere
to consider life and death circumstances.
Moments to decide whether to escape or submit.
In the end, he surrendered to God's will.
Willingly offered himself as a sacrifice.

Isaac responded in faith to an unfathomable request
from his father,
just as God's Son would one day do.

In the face of a rebellious world,
God tipped his hand using Abraham's experience
to model God's sacrifice of his own Son.
A visual premonition of the cross.
God tipped his hand using Isaac's experience
to model Jesus' complete submission to His Father's will.

Jesus' sacrificial act upon the cross bridged the gap of broken
relationship
between mankind and the Creator,
providing a redemptive avenue for you and me
to find peace in the arms of a loving God.
All that is required is an act of submission of our own.

"If anyone desires to come after Me,
let him deny himself,
and take up his cross, and follow Me."
—Matthew 16:24

AN ACT OF AUDACITY

Exodus 2:1-10

In the days of Joseph,
the Hebrew people lived a charmed life in Egypt.
Their farms, flocks and families flourished
under God's grace.
With Pharaoh's permission,
and Joseph's jurisdiction,
the Hebrew people prospered.

Joseph passed.
Centuries passed.
A new line of Pharaohs came to power
who cared nothing for Joseph's legacy.
God's man in Egypt vanished into the pages of distant history.

The new ruler grew anxious.
The Hebrew people were prolific,
growing in numbers with every passing generation.
Fearful of rebellion,
Pharaoh passed a horrid law.
Ordered his own soldiers to drown every
newborn Hebrew boy in the Nile River.
Many parents resisted.
Many were beaten.

Some were killed defending their sons.
Cries of mourning echoed throughout the
Hebrew camps for months without end.

*

Amram and Jochebed.
Living a nightmare
in a dusty, mud-brick home
on the outskirts of the royal city of Pithom.
An ordinary Hebrew family
of the tribe of Levi
suffered the deprivation of slaves.
Labored each day in the fields.

Two children born into a world of oppression.

Aaron.
Energetic and eager.
Articulate and able.
Serious and stubborn.

Miriam.
Precocious and perceptive.
Confident and clever.
Affectionate and adoring.

Bad enough that their two children
endured the hardships of slavery.
Jochebed felt a new stirring in her womb.
A third child on the way.
Ordinarily a blessed event.
Worthy of celebration.
No longer.
Pharaoh's edict turned the bliss of birth into
trepidation and terror.

*

Jochebed's water broke shortly after sunset.
The time had come.
Miriam, excited despite the danger,
ran quickly to fetch the midwife.
Jochebed bit down hard on the leather strap.
Anything to keep from crying out.
She wanted no one to know of the baby's birth,
at least until they discovered whether
God graced them with a little girl or boy.
Around midnight,
the family greeted a baby boy.
Bittersweet joy.

Jochebed had comforted too many mothers.
Friends who lost too many sons.

Determined to avoid what seemed inevitable,
the parents resolved to hide him from the Egyptians for as long
as possible.
An audacious act of civil disobedience.

Soldiers patrolled the village area every day,
busting through doors whenever they heard a baby cry.
Jochebed's ability to protect her son
depended on keeping him happy and content.
Without tears.

For three months,
Jochebed and Miriam seldom let the baby out of their arms.
Constantly cradled.
Lovingly rocked.
Soothed with songs
of Hebrew faith and joy.

Miriam cherished the baby.
Never took her eyes off him.
She imagined his eyes pleading with her.
"Love me!"
"Save me!"
"Protect me!"

She answered every whimper with whispers.
Every cry with caresses.
Every hurt with hugs.

Miriam's heart melted when he smiled.
Tears of joy welled in her eyes each time the boy
wrapped a tiny hand around her finger.
With each passing day, he became her life.
With each passing day,
she became his protector.

Miriam watched the sun rise.
She spent most of the night awake with the baby.
He spent a restless night,
as if he knew his days were numbered.
She cried as she prayed,
"Protect my brother."
"Let no one harm him."
"Give me strength."

*

As he grew,
the child's s sobs grew harder to muffle.
Just a matter of time before a passing guard
heard his cries and came to investigate.
In a decision no parents should ever have to make,
Amram and Jochebed did what they had to do
to give him a chance at life.
They had a plan.
Implausible and unlikely.
The small child's only hope.

In the cool of the evening,
under the faint light of the moon,
Jochebed and her daughter
spent the evening waterproofing a wicker basket
made from the reeds that grew upon the banks of the river.
Heating and stirring the bitumen
they purchased from a merchant two days before,
Jochebed slathered the basket with the thick, oily pitch.
Left it to dry overnight.

About an hour before the sun rose,
Jochebed woke Miriam.
She gently picked up her three-month-old son,
wrapped him loosely in a colorful blanket
she had woven in anticipation of his birth.

After feeding him and smothering him with kisses,
mother, left the house secretly,
followed closely by Miriam carrying the baby.
They stole between the houses,
avoiding the candlelight shining through half-opened doors.
They made their way to the river bank,
just outside the Pharaoh's palace,
in muted misery.

The tall reeds swayed in the light morning breeze,
effectively hiding the women from view of the Pharaoh's guards.

With a final kiss and cheeks wet with tears,
Jochebed placed her son in the basket,
pushed it into the water at the edge of the river.
Prayed for his safety and his life.
Unable to watch her act of desperation play out,
the heart-broken mother returned home deep in personal grief.
Miriam stayed behind,
hidden in the reeds
to see what would happen to the brother she loved.

The desert sun warmed the morning
beyond normal temperature.
Stifling and unbearable.
Yet, Miriam did not budge from her hiding place,
one eye fearfully on the palace gate,
one eye prayerfully on the papyrus basket.

Finally, about an hour after sunrise,
the riverside gate of the palace opened.
A group of six servants accompanied the Pharaoh's daughter
to bathe in the cool waters of the Nile.
As they splashed and played in the shallows,
the baby woke,
hungry and hot.
Quiet sobs grew in intensity.

The king's teenage daughter
heard the baby's cry,
sent a servant to investigate.
She returned to the side of her mistress,
basket and baby in hand.

Miriam tensed among the reeds.
The knife she secreted from her father's work bench clutched to
her chest.
At the slightest threat to her brother
she would attack.
She would die before she let them harm him.

The Pharaoh's daughter pulled back the blanket,
she looked in the eyes of a Hebrew child
who reached for her in hungry innocence.
Instead of calling for the palace guards,
Pharaoh's daughter crooned in sympathy.
Keenly aware of her father's order
demanding death for every newborn Hebrew boy,
the princess' heart opened in youthful compassion.
She determined to take the child home as her own.

Though dangerous to approach the Pharaoh's daughter without
permission,
Miriam crept closer to hear the conversation
between the Princess and her handmaidens.
One servant suggested the baby would die
without a wet nurse to care for him until weaned.

Miriam released a breath she didn't know she had been holding.
Dropped the knife in the mud at her feet.
The young girl boldly approached the Princess.
As Miriam neared, the servants
formed a protective ring around the royal daughter.
"Apologies, Mistress," said Miriam,
eyes averted, head down.
"While washing in the river,
I could not help but overhear your conversation.
I know a woman who just lost her baby.
I'm sure she would care for this little one."

Instead of recrimination,
Pharaoh's daughter looked gratefully at Miriam.
"Bring her to me."

*

What joy!
Stunning turn of events.

Pharaoh's daughter made the arrangements.
Jochebed would be paid to raise her child.
She would have time.
A few more years to shape the heart of her young son
before he became the Pharaoh's adopted grandson.
Years to teach the one
whom God had chosen before time to free his people.

"And they named him Moses."

Boldness

In childlike innocence,
Miriam acted boldly to protect her brother.
In doing so,
she taught a Godly lesson.
It's not always about us.

He could have it His way if He wanted.
Could act as master puppeteer pulling the strings of His Creation.
No free will.
Just make it happen His way.
That's not the way God works in the world He Created.

He needed a deliverer.
He chose Moses.
Long before his birth,
He chose Moses,
a child born under a Pharaoh's death sentence.

God knew.
In His desire to release His people from bondage,
God needed someone to carry his message to Egypt's tyrant.
God knew.

Pharaoh would never grant audience to a simple Hebrew shepherd
or even a dynamic Hebrew prophet.
But he could never turn away his prodigal grandson.

Moses had a role to play in God's master plan.
Pharaoh's murderous edict threw a kink in that plan.
If Pharaoh had his way,
who would deliver God's people from bondage?

God needed a deliverer for His deliverer.
He chose Miriam.
In response to Pharaoh's murderous intent,
He chose Miriam,
a young girl whose sibling love surpassed her dread.

God knew.
Miriam's protective spirit would allow no one to hurt the boy.
Not Pharaoh's soldiers.
Not Pharaoh's daughter.
Not Pharaoh himself.

Miriam hid in the reeds knowing nothing of God's plans
for Moses.
To her he was just her brother.
She saw no burning bush.
Experienced no divine dream.
Viewed no Godly vision to compel her forward.
No heavenly angel to tell her what to do.

She had only a stout heart
beating within an anxious and caring soul.

Miriam acted,
not out of a direct call from God,
but out of her love for her baby brother.
It wasn't about her.
It was about Moses.

History would belong to Moses.
God would do His work through this little one.
However, you would never know Moses
without first knowing Miriam.

*

It's not always about us.
It's often about the other.
Most of us will never be a Moses.
Most of us will never see a burning bush.
Encounter no angel.
Hear no voice.

Most of us will be more like Miriam.
Most of us will see just an opening,
an opportunity to do something on behalf of the other,
never knowing that one simple, random act,
might set in motion God's next great work.

Never knowing that a single word
might provide the encouragement the other needs
to approach his Burning Bush…
to listen to the Voice he hears…
to answer the call of God.

So, what does God require of those who
live in the shadows of the others who are called?

He asks for a stout heart that refuses to hide in the reeds
when the opportunity presents itself.
He asks us to refuse to dwell in the safety of self,
to act in selflessness.
When the frightened stay rooted in the mud,
He asks us to just lean in the right direction,
one simple movement that shows our willingness
to allow Him to guide our stumbling feet.

He asks for…
Nerve.
Daring.
Audacity.
Chutzpah.
He asks for boldness.

It's not always about us.
It's often about the other.

Let us then approach the throne of grace with boldness,
so that we may receive mercy
and find grace to help us in our time of need.
—Hebrews 4:16

THROW OUT THE FLEECE

Judges 6-7

Gideon.

Call him
concerned.

Purah watched the smoke from the smoldering fire
as it billowed slowly into the night sky,
one eye keenly upon the 300 men huddled around their tents,
the other eye on Gideon.

As he had for the past three months,
Purah sat next to the Israelite army's leader,
their backs resting against a smooth bolder.
Tonight, on the eve of battle,
he recognized the 1,000-yard stare from Gideon's deep-set eyes.
Same look seen in the eyes of countless soldiers
in the hours before any battle.

He was familiar with Gideon's look.
The man struggled inwardly more than most leaders.
Put up a good front with the men,
but he could never hide things from Purah.
Friends for too long.

Gideon's features reflected the strain.

Felt the heavy burden of command.

Agonized over the lack of real military training.

Riddled with self-doubt.

Worried about the impossible odds.

Waging a constant inner battle over

the uncertainty of God's call.

These thoughts consumed Gideon's heart and soul

every time he sat still long enough to think.

As the silence hung heavily between them

like the lingering smoke of the campfire,

Purah thought back to the day Gideon sought his help.

Remarkable tale.

Hard to believe.

Whatever transpired, it changed Gideon.

Convinced him to destroy idols to the false gods his people now

worshipped

and to organize an army to chase the Midianites

from the land of the Israelite people.

Purah looked into the dancing flames,

thinking about Gideon's transformation from a man of

laboring faith

to a man willing to lay everything in the hands of the

Almighty God.

*

Gideon.

Standing in an abandoned winepress

in the hill overlooking Gideon's acreage in the Jezreel

Valley below,

resting his weary arms on the winnowing fork,

wondering how his life had come to this.

Call him

inconsequential.

A simple farmer with a chip on his shoulder.

For the past seven harvests,

the hordes from the east flooded the valley.

As thick as a plague of locusts, they...

stole what they wanted,

trampled the grain,

ruined the crops,

destroyed the rest.

Resentful?

To be sure.

Bitter?

Without a doubt.

Indignant?

Every day.

Given the swarm of Midianite marauders
destroying his fields in the valley below,
he had a right to feel aggrieved.
But he was small in the grand scheme of things.

A son of the tribe of Manasseh...
Israel's most insignificant tribe.

A son of Abiezer...
Manasseh's weakest clan.
A son of Joash...
Least among his family.

Powerless to change his circumstances,
Gideon let his circumstances change his view of God.
Once,
devoted and dutiful.
Now,
disquieted and doubtful.

Fearful of the Midianites,
Gideon and his neighbors took to the hills,
frightened and frustrated,
to salvage what little of their crops could be saved.

Call him
cynical.

*

His life turned upside down, Gideon felt forsaken.
God's eyes looked elsewhere.
How else could one explain his current situation?
Deep within the recesses of the cliffs,
hiding from those would steal his livelihood.
Alone in an abandoned winepress.
Mumbling beneath his breath as he threshed.
Fuming as he separated the wheat from the chaff.

That was how the Lord's messenger found him.

The angel called him
"mighty warrior..."
A proud pronouncement.

Gideon heard
"mighty warrior..."
A sarcastic put down.

The angel said,
"The Lord be with you."
Words of omnipotence.

Gideon heard
"The Lord be with you."
Words of impotence.

Gideon reacted in the context of his current condition,
in the mood for a little argument.

"Now that you brought it up,
Where exactly has God gone?
Heard stories all my life.
Deliverance from Egypt.
Crossing the Red Sea.
Manna from heaven."

The people had gone from
miracles to Midianites.
Gideon's world perspective?
God abandoned Israel.
The nation stood powerless and alone.
He vented his frustration on the one God sent.

Wishing fervently for a change in his situation,
it never occurred to Gideon that he might be the
instrument of Israel's deliverance.

His limited faith and limited trust,
limited the possibilities of what God could do...
through him.

The man from Manasseh never saw this one coming.
The angel said,
*"Go, in the strength you have.
I am sending you to save Israel."*

Gideon's heart leapt even as his stomach fell.

Every possible excuse flowed from his lips.

"There is no strength here.

My people will not follow me.

My family is unimportant.

I'm the least among them.

Who would answer my trumpet call?

I can't do this!"

God never asked Gideon for strength he did not possess.

He asked Gideon to bring himself to the battle…

just as he was.

It would be enough because,

God promised,

"I'll be with you."

The angel's presence unsettled Gideon.

He calmed himself with a moment of

inner reflection and wistful thinking.

"Is God truly calling me…of all people?"

Collected an offering.

A little brisket.

A little bread.

A little broth.

The angel touched the food with his staff.

Consuming fire flared from the rock.

When the smoke cleared, the messenger was gone.

The miraculous sign brought Gideon to his feet.

He stared unmoving as the charred food smoldered on the stone.

Gideon struggled within his own skin.

Doubted his abilities.

Instead of trusting the Father in the task ahead,

he focused on his own insecurities.

The least of Manasseh, offered so little.

In God's hands,

would Gideon's little be enough?

Call him

chosen.

*

Gideon.

Filled with courage.

Inspired by God's sign.

Recruited an army to gather at Mt. Gilead.

32,000 willing men of Israel,

faced 120,000 nomadic tribesmen.

Time and the overwhelming odds stole the farmer's confidence.
Purah saw the first vacant stare in Gideon's eyes this day.

Gideon.

Filled with reservations,

anxious about everything,

growing weak in the knees.

Appealed to God for another sign...or two.

Dry fleece...Wet grass.

Dry grass...Wet fleece.

The astonishing patience of God nudged Gideon down His

chosen path.

Every time he felt overwhelmed,

every time he felt unworthy,

every time he wanted to walk away,

he requested reassurance from the Father.

God answered Gideon's requests

for no other reason but to strengthen Gideon's grit.

Offered Godly reassurance

to break down Gideon's reluctance.

Every answered test took away Gideon's excuses.

Bolstered his wavering confidence.

Gideon returned to camp and prepared again for battle.

*

Lest anyone should boast in victory
and fail to recognize God's work,
the Almighty told Gideon to reduce his numbers.
God now put Gideon and his soldiers to the test.
As they sipped water from the stream,
God sent the fearful and the less vigilant home.
Israel's 32,000 warriors dwindled to 300.
Alert and aware.
Best of the best.
Israel's first special forces unit.

Gideon,
constantly mindful of the fleece,
prepared to fight.
Yet again, under pressure,
Gideon's mettle melted.
Embraced his inner coward.
Buckled knees.
Puckered mouth…Dry as dust.

Purah read his face.
Sensed the dread.
Observed another vacant look.
300 against so many.
Am I doing the right thing?
The second thoughts of every military leader on the eve of battle.

God gave Gideon one last sign,
one last word of encouragement.

Before the moon rose,
Gideon conducted a late night reconnaissance mission,
sneaking to the edge of the enemy's camp,
with Purah by his side.
Together, they eavesdropped on a quiet conversation
among the teenaged Midianite guards.
They spoke of impending doom,
defeat at the hands of Gideon and the Israelite army.

Shadowed in darkness,
hiding behind a bush,
deep in enemy territory,
Gideon smiled in calm assurance.
Returning to the camp, he
worshipped the God of his deliverance.
Readied his troops.

"*Jehovah-Shalom*,"
"God of Peace,"
stilled Gideon's heart.
Granted peace to the nation of Israel.

Call him
convinced.

*

Early in the morning,
in the darkest hours right before sunrise,
Gideon and his 300 surrounded the enemy camp
armed with
Weapons of Mass Confusion.

Each man gathered a trumpet,
a jar and a torch.
As one,
300 trumpets sounded.
300 jars smashed.
300 torches shattered the darkness
A mighty shout in chorus,
"For the Lord and for Gideon."

An enemy scattered in chaos.
Chased and crushed.

Call him
Committed.

Call him
Gideon.

Dependence

Gideon.
So ordinary.
No one special.
No family prestige.
No personal power.
No political position.

Gideon behaved a lot like us.
Lived a lot like us.
Getting by day by day.
Doing what we have to do.
Providing for our families.
Clinging to faith,
battered by life's circumstances.

A still, small voice whispers,
"I am sending you."
We fixate on the obstacles,
amassing before us like a horde of Midianites.
We offer only excuses.
"Not me.
I am unable.
Too small.
Too insignificant.
Not going to happen."

Nevertheless,

Give Gideon credit.

God called.

With little reason to believe in himself,

Gideon answered...

not without hesitation,

not without question,

but he answered.

In the end,

faith need not be bold to be authentic.

Faith need not be strong to be useful.

Faith, whatever germ of it exists in us,

requires only that our will

yields to His will.

Fully trusting.

Completely dependent.

With just a shade of scorn,

we raise our eyebrows every time Gideon asks God for a sign.

"O you of little faith!"

As if our faith ran deeper.

We question the commitment of others who grapple with doubts

and fears.

"O you of little faith!"

As if we never question God's sanity.

When nothing makes sense,
when the odds seem stacked against us,
when everything challenges our long-held
beliefs about God and ourselves,
we must become faith-dependent.

The human heart often struggles in understanding God's will.
When we desire to be where God wants us to be,
and we're not sure where we stand,
can it be wrong to lay out our fleece?
Not to test God,
but in a quest for our own reassurance
from the One who knows our limitations and
calls us in spite of who we are.

So,
lay out your fleece.
Check for clarity.

Am I here today where you need me to be?
Let me know.

Have I followed your path?
Give me peace.

Am I pushing my own agenda or following Your lead?
Give me a sign.

That testing works as long as we recognize the signs God provides.

An angel from heaven.

Flames from a rock.

A wet fleece, dry grass.

Wet grass, a dry fleece.

All proved insufficiently awe-inspiring

for Gideon to take God completely at His word.

How ironic!

A man of halting faith finally

gathered the courage he needed from the

frightened musings of a worried warrior.

Not from the miraculous,

but from the mundane.

Go ahead.

Lay out your fleece.

But sooner or later

the time for fleece-laying

gives way to time to act in trust.

We claim His promise of power

amid our human weakness.

"I can do all things through Christ

who strengthens me"

—Philippians 4:13

MORE THAN A LOVE STORY

Ruth 1-4

The heavy cloak pulled tightly around her shoulders
did little to block the biting cold of the north wind.
Matched the chill in her heart and
the icy emptiness in her soul.
Standing at the top of the dusty plateau looking west into Judah,
she saw the walls of Jericho on the slopes climbing steeply
from the banks of the Dead Sea.
Judah was home.
It had been too long.
Too long since her husband, Elimelech, and two children
crossed the Jordan River east into Moab
to a place where the drought had not torched the soil.
Too long.

Naomi embraced her two daughters-in-law.
They were family.
They were alone.
She found it difficult to say goodbye.

Tears flowed freely down her cheeks.
Death had its victory.
Sorrow ruled the day and night.
She had lost too much.

Ten years to the month,
Naomi's beloved husband died in her arms,
creating a void in Naomi's heart
more expansive than the heavens.
Pouring her life into the lives of her two sons and their new wives,
she buried her grief behind an emotional wall.
Through their joy she found each passing day
less painful than the one before.

Until the wall came crashing down.
A fever claimed the eldest son;
her youngest a few weeks later.
Profound misery.
Heart shattered and crushed.
A life once blessed now seemed cursed.
Empty of bliss.
Filled with bitterness.

She saw the same desolate look in the eyes of her daughters-in-law.
Their lives had been irrevocably changed in ways
they were only beginning to understand.
Naomi had witnessed life's unfairness and
understood far better than most.
The world was unkind to those without a husband.
Marginalized its widows.
Without family support and shelter,
they would struggle to survive.

Naomi turned toward Bethlehem
to return to her own people,
her daughters-in-law huddled by her side.
The three of them.
Financially destitute.
Emotionally desolate.
Physically drained.

Naomi prodded them to return to their own families,
hoping they would find peace and rest among their kin.
Reluctantly,
Orpah walked away.
Willingly,
Ruth begged to stay,
unable to leave Naomi alone in her distress.

Brushing aside her own heartache,
Ruth's heart opened to the one she loved as a mother.
Clutching the hem of Naomi's skirt,
through tear-filled eyes,
Ruth whispered,

"Don't urge me to leave you or to turn back from you.
Where you go, I will go.
Where you stay, I will stay.
Your people will be my people.
Your God my God.
Where you die, I will die,
and there I will be buried."

Supported by mutual and absolute devotion,
they walked resolutely toward Bethlehem.
An Israelite woman.
Her Moabite daughter-in-law.
Toward an uncertain future.
Arm in arm.

*

Naomi and Ruth
settled on the fringe of family
in the hills outside of Bethlehem.
Self-imposed isolation.

"Call me 'bitter,'" Naomi insisted.
"The Lord afflicted me; brought misfortune upon me."
Hopelessness ruled her life.
Tainted her outlook.
Skewed her perspective.
While Naomi wallowed in despair,
Ruth eked out a meager existence for both of them,
depending daily on the generosity of others.

*

The barley blew gently in the breeze,
ripe and ready for harvest.
Across the roughly terraced hills farmers moved slowly
clipping the heads of grain from the stalk,
tossing them in the baskets they carried on their hips.

A rag-tag collection of the poor,
the lame,
the widowed,
the disconnected
followed behind the harvesters.
These unfortunate ones gathered up and carried home
any grain dropped by those who reaped.
It was the Gleaning.
Social welfare of the day.
Physical provision for those who could not provide for themselves.

Ruth joined the outcasts each day,
bringing home to Naomi the seeds of their survival.
As constant as the rising sun,
Ruth provided for Naomi.
A labor of love.

*

Boaz.
Distantly related to Naomi's husband.
A man of standing and wealth.
Kind and generous.
Compassionate and charitable.
Righteous and respected.
A good and decent man.

As Boaz walked among his fields observing the harvest,
a young woman caught his eye.
Busy.
Hard working.
Attractive.
Working among the outcasts.

Captivated, he asked the overseer to whom she belonged.
When told of her work ethic and her
family devotion to Naomi,
Boaz granted her privileges in his fields.

Fed her.

Quenched her thirst.

Dropped a little more grain at her feet,

as a token of esteem and appreciation.

Ruth returned home as the sun set,

exhaustion eased by excitement.

A quick mother-to-daughter talk.

Intrigued by the day's developments.

For the first time in months,

Naomi caught a glimmer of light amid the darkness.

"God has not walked out on us after all!"

Could she dare hope?

*

Levirate marriage.

A Jewish legal concept of family responsibility.

A family's responsibility to a widow.

A kinsman-redeemer.

It was the law.

In the wayward state of Hebrew faith

few honored the precept,

ignoring the plight of women like Naomi and Ruth.

*

Naomi knew Boaz as kinsman-redeemer.
Despair lifted from her heart
like the morning mist in the warmth of the rising sun.
Her love for Ruth, her dreams for Ruth,
broke down the bleak barriers of her own loneliness.

Naomi rejoiced in God's hand at work.
The Provider opened a door.
Righteous and good-hearted,
Boaz was an answered prayer.
She told Ruth…

Clean up.
Dab on a little perfume.
Dress up.
Wait until he sleeps.
Lie at his feet.
The first step in requesting his favor.

*

Boaz finished threshing for the evening.
Bushels of barley lined the walls of the stone shelter.
After dinner and a little wine shared with his servants,
he retreated to the edge of the camp.
Wrapped in the warmth of his cloak,
he slept the deep slumber of a contented heart.

Ruth quietly entered the campsite.
Curled up at the feet of Boaz,
a traditional sign of her willingness to commit her life to him.
A simple act that put her future in his hands.

Boaz woke in the middle of the night,
noticed a woman resting at the foot of his pallet.
Ruth identified herself in a hushed conversation.
"Spread the corner of your cloak around me."
Her way of asking Boaz to take her as a wife.

Much depended on his reaction.
Touched by her sincerity.
Flattered by her request.
Boaz sent her home with a promise.
He would not rest until he
fulfilled his obligation as
kinsman-redeemer.

A hastily arranged meeting at the city gate.
Boaz opened negotiations with Elimelech's closest relative.
Though willing to profit from Naomi's land,
the man stopped short of taking Ruth as his wife.
Nothing to be gained by it.
Abdicated his spiritual responsibility.
Boaz paid the price of redemption and
married Ruth.

*

The colorful shawl hung loosely around her shoulders
as the warm southern breeze brushed the hair from her face.
Matched the warmth in her heart and
the deep contentment in her soul.
Standing on the crest of the hill looking west into the
Rephaim Valley.
Green in fertile splendor.
Naomi cradled her grandson in her arms.
New life.
She smiled at the soft noises he made,
as she stretched out her arm to embrace Ruth.
She was home.
It had been too long.
Too long.

In the days to come,
Naomi found a place in the
home created by Boaz and Ruth.
No longer alone.
No longer bitter.
Delightful again.

Together with the women of Bethlehem,
Naomi rejoiced in God's blessings.
For a new home.
For a new family.
For Ruth's sustaining love.
For personal redemption.

Redemption

On the surface
a story of faithfulness and fidelity.
Charming.
Comfortable.
A 1940s Hollywood love story.
Little more than an overused wedding vow.

"Where you go,
I will go."

It is more.
Much more.
A biblical revelation.
Deep in measure and meaning.
Hidden treasures.
Heavenly truths.

Without question,
Ruth tells a story of family devotion.
Of self-giving love.
Of God's compassion toward the
hurting and the lost.

Ruth,
God's instrument of empathy to Naomi.
Boaz,
His instrument of restoration to Ruth.

The book begins and ends with Naomi.
A transformation from
bitterness to blessing.

*

Naomi.
Torn apart by the loss of a husband,
the loss of both sons.
Devastated.
She withdraws within herself,
wallowing in her personal grief.
Ancient sorrow suffers as keenly as our own.

Ruth provides the example of
Godly compassion.

To the hurting we say,
Where you go, I will go.
We will walk together.

To the helpless we say,
Where you stay, I will stay.
You will not be alone.

To the hopeless we say,
Your God my God.
We will feel His presence always.

*

Boaz provides the example of Godly restoration.

For those who are hungry we say,
"Have some bread."
I will meet your physical requirements.

To those who are needy we say,
"I will do for you all you ask."
You will not want for anything.

To those who are lost we say,
"I am your kinsman-redeemer."
My home is your home.

*

As instructive as Ruth and Boaz may be
in how we as Christians should live,
the Book of Ruth
begins and ends with Naomi.

It is not simply a story of devotion
between two women.
It is not simply a May/September romance
between a young widow and an older man.
Is a story of one woman's redemption.

Throughout the Old Testament
redemption and deliverance
are acts of grace of a loving God toward
the nation of Israel.
Through the circumstances of Naomi's life,
deliverance is personal.
Restoration is personal.
Redemption is personal.

Redemption.
Offered by a loving Father.
Demonstrated by God's people.
Our lives need not stay mired in the swamp of loneliness.

Through a melding of God's maneuvering
and faithful human choices,
we need not remain trapped in the cycle of despair
no matter what devastation falls upon us.

Redeemed!
How I love to proclaim it!
Redeemed by the blood of the Lamb!

For all have sinned and fall short of the glory of God,
and all are justified freely by his grace
through the redemption that came by Christ Jesus.
—Romans 3:23-24

THE SLING AND THE STONE

I Samuel 17

Philistines to the south.
Israelites to the north.
Surrounded by stunted Terebinth trees.
Separated by a fertile valley.
Split by a babbling brook,
a young boy's armory.

Battle lines arrayed in typical formation.
Nervous soldiers stared across the valley,
neither side eager to fight when death waited.

A giant stalked the valley between them.
Goliath of Gath.
Loathsome in appearance.
Fearsome in stature.
9 feet, 9 inches tall.
Shoulders broad. Muscles ripped.

Clad in a heavy helmet.
Covered in armor scaled in bronze…
armor that, by itself, easily outweighed any Hebrew warrior.
Goliath paced the battlefield.

Each movement of his body shimmered in the morning sun,
reflecting sunlight into the eyes of his opponents.
Disorienting.
Disconcerting.
Disheartening.

Armed to the teeth.
Javelin strapped across his back.
Sword sheathed around his waist.
Spear, as thick as a weaver's beam,
held loosely in his mammoth hand.
A servant to carry his shield.

His deep voice echoed from the depths of Sheol.
Taunting and insulting the Israelite army.
Angry arrogance.
Cursed their fathers.
Damned their mothers.
Insulted their God.
"Forget the armies," Goliath screamed.
Send one warrior to fight.
Just one.
Giant to man.
Man wins.
Philistines will serve Israel.
Giant wins.
Israel will serve Philistines.

Israel's king and all its soldiers shuddered.

None stepped forward.

Day after day,

Goliath goaded.

Day after day,

King Saul and his men grumbled.

None stepped forward.

*

Saul.

First king of Israel.

Providentially appointed by God.

Publicly anointed by Samuel

to lead God's people.

Saul's ego got in the way.

The king no longer listened to God or His prophet.

Saul turned his heart from God.

God turned his eyes toward

Jesse's son.

A shepherd boy from Bethlehem.

Ephraim's new hope.

The future king of Israel.

Youngest of eight brothers.

David.

Sheep herder in his father's fields.

Servant in the king's court

where his music and poetry

calmed the king's troubled soul.

Young and eager.

Handsome in a rugged sort of way.

Red-haired and red-faced

from exposure to the sun.

A young man after God's own heart.

A Spirit-filled heart.

Providentially, appointed by God.

Privately, anointed by Samuel.

David embraced the promises that Saul squandered.

One day, he would be king,

but not this day.

*

David's brothers had been called to service.

Foot soldiers in the King's army.

Jesse called David from his work,

sending him with a care package for his older brothers.

He arrived on the hillside just outside of Azekah.

The army positioned for battle.

David could almost smell the fear.

He pushed his way through the ranks of soldiers,

finding his brothers amid the thousands.

They stood prepared for battle, but rooted in fright,
silent as the stones that littered the hillside,
facing the Philistine army as they had done for 40 days.

David watched in shocked amazement
as the Philistine battle lines parted.
Into the lush valley of Elah stomped Goliath
as he did every morning,
hurling the same insults,
the same curses,
the same slurs,
toward the Hebrew soldiers and their God.

As he came forward,
the Israelite warriors involuntarily stepped back.
"Man to man," he yelled again.
David stood among the soldiers,
astonished as no one answered his challenge.

"Who is this Philistine that defies the God of Israel?"
Grown men looked away:
embarrassed,
emasculated,
powerless.

Hearing that someone at last
answered the challenge,
Saul ordered his captains to bring the volunteer to his tent.

Expecting a warrior,
the servants brought him a boy.
Expecting a soldier,
the servants brought him a musician.
Expecting a fighter,
the servants brought him a poet.

Saul studied Israel's would-be "champion."
Slowly shaking his head,
he rubbed his sweaty forehead.
Elbow resting wearily on the arm of his throne,
Saul looked David over from head to toe.

"Too small.
Too weak.
Too inexperienced," Saul said.
"You will surely die."

The thought of death had not crossed David's mind until
that moment.
Saul's declaration shattered his sense of invincibility.
Goliath suddenly became more than a disembodied voice
echoing from the battlefield.
David closed his eyes and saw the giant striking a warrior's pose.
Flesh and bone.
Muscle and sinew.
Strong and battle-tested.
Death cloaked in a Giant's skin.

Saul's words reverberated
"Too small.
Too weak."
A momentary flicker of self-doubt fluttered through David's heart
before God rekindled its blaze.

The young shepherd thought back to
rocky hills surrounding Bethlehem,
seeing a blood-soaked bear dying at his feet,
its throat slashed by David's knife.
Thought back to a night under a full moon.
Seeing a lion breathe its last shallow breath,
pinned to the ground with David's sword.
In his arms,
the rescued sheep.
On his lips,
a grateful prayer to a protective God.

Saul spoke the truth.
On his own,
David was no match for Goliath.
"Too small.
Too weak."
But he was far from untested.

For in David's past,
God proved himself as
his Source of Strength.
His Protector.
His Deliverer.

Confident and trusting.
David knew the past was proof
of God's presence.
The Philistine would fall before David and his God.

Declining the king's ill-fitting, heavy armor,
David grabbed only his walking stick and his sling.
As he walked toward the Elah Valley, into the very
shadow of death,
the soldiers stepped aside for the shepherd.

David crossed the brook.
Selected five smooth stones.
Placed them in his shepherd's bag.

*

Goliath sneered as he saw the Israelite lines separate.
"About time," he grumbled under his breath.
Then Goliath laughed in derision and grew angry.
His challenge had been answered
by little more than a child.

"Are all men of Israel cowards
that you would send a boy to fight for you?"
More insults.
More curses.
More threats.
Bones to wild animals.
Flesh to birds.
Arrogant.
Unimpressed.

David scanned the hillsides.
While clouds floated lazily across the morning sky,
he smelled the smoke from the early morning campfires.
Heard the buzz of bees flitting from flower to flower.
Felt the breeze brush the hair from his face.
Sensed the peace of God's spirit in his heart,
and the power of God's might in his hand.

David slowly turned his gaze toward the giant.
Stood his ground.
Unfazed by size,
spear,
sword
or shield.

Measuring the familiar weight of his sling in his hand,

David snapped the leather strap against his tunic.

Took a deep, calming breath.

Mumbled a short prayer to the Father in Heaven.

He slipped his hand into the bag,

feeling the texture and hardness of the stones,

fingers tightening around the smoothest one.

With assured conviction David spoke confidently to Goliath.

"My God, whom you defy,

will deliver you into my hands.

You will die.

Lose your head.

Your army crushed.

At the end of the day,

all the earth will know there is a God in Israel."

With the outcome predetermined in his heart,

David's confidence unnerved and angered the giant even more.

Goliath charged forward in fury.

David walked forward in faith.

A single stone slid quickly into the sling.

The shepherd twirled it over his head faster and faster.

With perfect timing, David let go of one strap,

sending the stone toward its intended target

with precise and deadly aim.

The river rock struck Goliath just below the rim of his helmet.

The giant took three long steps before he

collapsed to his knees and toppled forward…

dead before he hit the ground.

The cheers and jeers of the Philistine army ceased.

Stunned silence fell upon the battlefield.

David snatched the giant's sword.

With all the force he could muster,

Goliath's head rolled.

Cheers erupted from the Israelite hillside,

as despair gave way to victory.

Seeing their champion vanquished,

the Philistines fled before God's army.

Leaving their dead and dying.

Bones to wild animals.

Flesh to birds.

Stretching from the Valley of Elah

to the Great Sea.

In the days that followed,

songs were sung.

"Saul has slain his thousands.

David his tens of thousands."

Confidence

"All the earth will know there is a God in Israel."
That's what David told Goliath.
Complete confidence.

When the stone hit,
as the giant fell,
Goliath discovered what David already knew,
an undeniable truth embedded in that last fraction of
consciousness.
There is a God in Israel.

When the stone hit,
as the giant fell,
David's brothers, by blood and by bond...
those standing fearfully on the hillside...
discovered what David already knew.
There is a God in Israel.

David walked confidently in the Lord.

The challenge before us...
Discovering with conviction what David already knew.
There is a God in Israel.

Our Israel.

Our heart.

Protector.

Defender.

Victor.

How easy it is to trust in abstract!

David's story leads to a false complacency.

See giant.

Slay giant.

Sounds so easy.

So we sing...

"Onward, Christian soldiers,

Marching as to war..."

Until...

the battle lines part.

The world strides into the valley, armed to the teeth.

The world insults.

The world taunts.

The world curses.

The world challenges.

The music fades.
The march falters.
We freeze, paralyzed with fear.
Confronted by our giants we stand on the hillside...

Timorous of spirit.
Timid of soul.
Tempted to scatter.

Where do we find our confidence?
How do we stand like David?

David's confidence in God existed long before
he walked into the valley
in full view of his king,
his brothers
and his enemies.

David's confidence in God was grounded years earlier when
he walked alone in the mountains
with no one watching
except a lion
and a bear.

Experiencing God's deliverance even once in life's smallest battles
allows us to draw upon our history with Him.
Allows us to fight the next fight.
Confidence comes from knowing God.
Intimately.

Yesterday's encounter.
Today's hope.
Yesterday's experience.
Today's confidence.

He doesn't ask us to stand by ourselves.
He doesn't ask us to become something we are not.
He doesn't ask us to put on another's armor and another's
authority.
He asks only that when the trials come,
we arm ourselves with what He provides along the way…
His sling.
His stones.

We can stand with Him
no matter how many giants challenge us.
Confident in the outcome.

Somewhere along the way,
we discover what David already knew.
There is a God in Israel
There is a God in our hearts.
He is enough.

This is the confidence we have in approaching God:

that if we ask anything according to his will, he hears us.

And if we know that he hears us—whatever we ask—

we know that we have what we asked of him.

—I John 5:14-15

LIE DOWN WITH LIONS

Daniel 6:1-24

The old man stood bare-chested in the desert sun,
stripped of his royal robe and sash.
The sand swirled around his sandals in the hot, zephyr wind.
All eyes in the palace focused on him.
Nearby, women warbled a continuous, high-pitched wail.
Mourning.
Death paced wildly below.
Enemies bowed in mock regret
at how the mighty one had fallen,
privately smirking in pride at the
clever way in which they sealed his fate.

Standing in front of the barred gate
covering the pit below,
the elderly one heard the deep, resonant growling.
Six lions caged in the darkness.
Terrifying sounds that made the guards around him flinch.
Instinctively, the animals sensed
the impending feast awaiting them.
Jumping onto the side of the stone-walled cavern.
Scratching for a claw-hold on the rock.
Ravenous hunger wrapped in matted lion skin.

It surprised him!

He was not afraid.

Impending death buried in the distant recesses of his mind.

Long, full life.

Clear conscience.

Complete trust.

His life ever in the hands of

his Lord,

his God.

No different this day.

In a moment of clarity,

in a lifetime of faith.

He knew.

The future belonged to God.

His time.

His will.

His way.

In those last moments of private reflection,

he lifted his eyes to heaven

and prayed.

At peace with himself.

When life seemed hopeless,

Daniel prayed.

A prayer of praise.

A petition seeking strength.

When life seemed hopeless,
God answered.
In vivid imagery of personal recollection,
God reminded Daniel of His absolute faithfulness.
His life intertwined with Israel's history.
What act of God brought him to this?

*

For its disobedience and disinterest,
God, the Father, removed His hand of protection.
War followed.
Judah fell to Babylon.
Fell hard.
Fell off the map.

Staggering loss of life.
Stinging loss of national identity.
God's people
belonged to Babylon.
Lock, stock and Menorah.

*

Daniel.

Descendant of David.

Prince of Judah.

Youthful.

Physically fit.

Intelligent. Skilled.

Wise. Gifted.

Quick-witted.

Teachable.

Trustworthy.

Without corruption.

Daniel.

Captured and carried away.

Enslaved in a foreign land.

Servant to the pagan king.

This was not how he planned his life.

But Daniel knew only one way to live…

He *"purposed to do right."*

He chose to live life in response to God's call

for principled and purposeful living.

Dedication.

Service.

Prayer.

Courage of Convictions.

No guile.

No deceit.

Day in.

Day out.

Faithfully serving his master, the king.

Faithfully serving his Lord, the King of Kings.

Years later, another Son of David taught,

"Give to Caesar what is Caesar's and unto God what is God's."

Daniel lived that way.

Integrity...

in all aspects of life.

in all times of life.

in all circumstances of life.

God opened doors of opportunity.

Daniel walked through each door determined

to testify to the power and glory of the God of Judah.

Regal visions.

Royal nightmares.

Handwriting on the wall.

God revealed His truth through Daniel's interpretations.

Gifted in wisdom and understanding,

the king found Daniel 10 times the equal of his greatest advisors.

*

Embittered political operatives
passed over for promotion
failed to see the hand of God in Daniel's life.
They saw only…
Daniel,
the interloper.
Daniel,
the inferior.
Daniel,
a royal pain in their aspirations.

That was where the trouble started.

In a masterful stroke of political intrigue and personal
back stabbing,
they plotted to end Daniel's influence on the king.
Those who manipulate disdain those
who live by principle and purpose.
Such is the way of evil men.

Character assassination would not work.
Daniel's life was too clean.
Play off Daniel's devotion to his God.
Use his own faithfulness against him.
They approached the king with lies and deceit.

*

King Darius.
Decent man.
Ego bigger than Babylon.
Vain? At times.
Arrogant? On occasion.
The advisors whispered in his ear.
The gods needed a holiday.
Declare a 30-day moratorium on prayer to the gods.
All gods and all men...except, of course...
Marduk's favorite.

Darius.
"Man of the Month."

Sounded appealing in a narcissistic kind of way.

A simple decree.
Pray only to Darius
or die!

They knew.
Daniel would kneel before his God.
Prayer was his routine.
Every day.
Like clockwork.

He could not stop.

Not for 30 days.

Not for Darius.

Not to save his own life.

Daniel knew.

They would watch.

Prayer was his second nature.

Like breathing in and breathing out.

He could not stop.

Not for 30 days.

Not for Darius.

Not to save his own life.

To stop praying was death.

To keep praying was death.

So, Daniel did what Daniel always did.

Daniel prayed.

Prayed for wisdom.

Prayed for faithfulness.

Prayed for strength.

Prayed for those who lurked in the shadows,

banking on Daniel's faithfulness to his God.

When the inevitable happened,

when Daniel faced Jerusalem and prayed,

the king's advisors tattled.

Hopping in mock distress before the king,
they exposed Daniel's "guilt."
The king realized too late he had been duped.

The law.
Immutable.
Unchangeable.

Daniel.
Prince of Judah.
Prince among Babylon's princes
must die.
No exceptions.

*

Daniel's heart caught the change in the tenor of the crowd.
A dark cloud cast a shadow across the city.
The drums,
signaling the time of punishment,
struck a final beat.

Silence descended on the courtyard like a heavy mist.
Deafening stillness broken by a petrifying growl
released by the alpha beast below.
The executioner hurled Daniel into the lion's den.
The roar of the big cats reached a crescendo for several minutes.
Bloodcurdling.
Spine-chilling.

Inside the palace walls,

the king pressed his palms against his ears.

Nothing lessened the terrifying growl of the lions.

Each primal snarl tore at his heart.

More horrific was the deathly quiet that ensued.

The king prayed to the God of Judah,

to Daniel's God,

ironically violating his own decree.

*

Deep in the lion's den,

God sealed the mouths of the hungry animals.

Though restless and ravenous,

the animals paced the small cistern for hours,

never moving against Daniel.

Into the cold night,

Daniel continued to pray.

Man and beast grew weary.

Then, he lay down with the lions.

Slept the peaceful sleep of an innocent man,

protected by Yahweh.

*

In contrast,

King Darius did not rest.

Daybreak finally shimmered through the morning haze.
Beside himself with grief,
the king ran to the lion's den,
ordering the guard to lower a rope.
Hoping against hope,
Darius called for Daniel.

"Did your God deliver you?"

The response from the recesses of the cavern below thrilled
his heart.
Acknowledging the king's authority,
The old man replied with customary respect,
reflecting his personal integrity,
"Live forever, my king.
My God sent his angel.
I am innocent in His sight and in yours."

The king honored Daniel from that day forward
and declared the God of Judah,
the Eternal, Living God.

Integrity

Think about Daniel.
Descendant of David.
One of the princes of Judah.
The world was his oyster.
For a time.
Once a leader.
Now a slave.
Exiled far from home.

Life changed dramatically.
Yet Daniel wasted no time bemoaning his fate,
shaking his fist to the heavens,
wondering why God deserted him.

Instead,
he *purposed to do right...*
always.
For no other reason but to honor his Creator,
to let his life testify to the
glory and greatness of his Father, God.
Given his circumstances,
it was not an easy thing to do.

Daniel teaches us.
To live out the courage of our convictions
requires constant connection with our Lord.
Daniel prayed daily.
Prayed without ceasing.
Prayed as a pattern of life.
He talked to God.
He listened to God.
He learned from God.
What he learned,
he applied.

In a deliberate choice,
he purposed to do right.
Our ability to stay in constant communication with the Father
enables us to make right choices,
to live a disciplined and resolute life.

Daniel's life teaches another deeply valuable lesson.
Ours ought to be a living faith
actively at work in the world around us,
not cloistered safely behind the walls of worship.

Daniel's trust in God remained evident in the way he
served his king,
the way he did his job.
Faith dictated how he worked.

To those in authority over him,
he offered respect.
An honest day's work for an honest day's pay.
If asked to carry a pack a mile,
he carried it two.
A visual testimony
to the power of God in his life.

It should be no different for us.
We live and work in a secular world.
God would have us respect every employer and every worker.
Demonstrate the teachings of Christ in our behavior.
Match completely each day the things we say
with the things we do.
Practice what we preach.

Integrity.
High moral character.
Completeness.
Honest and incorruptible.
Purpose without pretense.
Trust without treachery.
Service without selfishness.

Daniel understood what it meant to be a
representative of the Father in his world.

He understood what it meant to live life in such a way
as to be wholly distinct from the lives of those around you.
His life of faithfulness,
his enduring work ethic and
his principled daily walk
left his enemies with
"no grounds for charges against him."

May it ever be so for us.

*"Let your light shine before men
that they may see your good deeds and
praise your Father in heaven."*
—Matthew 5:16

Last Boat to Tarshish

Jonah 1:1-4:11

The stranger boarded the last boat to Tarshish.

Incognito.
Cloak pulled tightly around his shoulders.
Face hooded and hidden.

Mysterious.
With a furtive glance to the east,
he slipped below deck without a word.

Secretive.
"Paid his fare," the Captain said.
"Don't ask questions.
Let him be."

Enigmatic.
Jonah, a man of God,
a fugitive fighting a deep burden of guilt.

How did it come to this?

*

Israel.

His home. His country.

Ruled by Jeroboam II,

sinful and self-centered like its king,

but regaining military strength.

Misinterpreted God's leniency

for God's approval.

Nineveh.

A great city. Powerful and ruthless.

Capital of cruelty.

Wicked and wasteful.

Brutal and bloodthirsty.

Arrogant and aggressive.

Jonah.

Israel personified.

Zealously patriotic.

Lover of his country and its people.

His people.

National pride blinded faith.

Quick to offer God's grace to the Hebrews.

Slow to offer God's grace to an ancient enemy.

Provincial.

Predictable.

Prejudiced.

Jonah wrapped his existence in the Hebrew's
special relationship with God,
the Father.
He lived in a resurgent nation
under imminent threat from the dreaded Assyrians.
That was his world.
Entitled.
Infallible.
In denial.

*

God said to Jonah,
"Go to Nineveh.
Cry out against it for I have seen their wickedness."

It sounded simple enough.
Grab your passport,
take a trip.
Admonish their sin.
Call them to turn from evil.
Show God's mercy.
Encourage them.
Help them survive.

But Jonah heard,

"My blessing is for all people...

even the enemies of the Chosen...

even those who rejected the God of Moses and Abraham...

even those who kill for the sport of killing...

even those you despise with every fiber of your being.

Go!

Let them know I love them."

Jonah knew the voice of God when he heard it.

He heard,

but refused to listen.

God asked too much!

Assyria.

An historic and mortal enemy.

Nothing good can come from Nineveh.

Forget this!

So, he slipped away in the dead of night,

walked in solitude to Joppa,

boarded the last boat to Tarshish.

Jonah,

the Father's instrument of salvation to a lost city,

turned his back on his mission.

In response to a call from the Father, Creator,

Jonah opted for a cruise of

disobedience and defiance.

*

Tarshish.

Not the end of the world,

but you could see it from there.

Jonah paid his fare.

Settled in his cabin for a pleasant cruise across the Great Sea.

To the far corner of the earth.

Far from Nineveh.

As far from God, as a man could go.

A futile attempt to avoid God's call.

A storm of biblical proportions erupted!

A battered and shattered ship tossed on the waves,

its crew desperately fighting to survive.

While Jonah slept fitfully in the hold,

restless in his dreams,

the gale outside raged as wildly as

the tempest within his heart.

Unanswered prayers to unhearing gods.
Desperate for deliverance,
they cast lots to cast blame.
Jonah drew the short straw.
The weight of the storm
fell squarely on his shoulders.

Tossed overboard in a last ditch effort to placate the vengeful gods,
Jonah embraced Death,
finding it infinitely more desirable
than embracing Nineveh.

Into the waves and into the belly of the monstrous fish.
Three days and three nights Jonah wallowed in his misery,
until he had a change of heart.
Sort of.

"Salvation is from the Lord,"
he half-heartedly prayed.
Yet, Jonah experienced God's forgiveness,
half dead, washed up on a beach,
bathed in a disgusting pool of fish vomit.

*

With the reluctant heart,
God's prophet admitted defeat and
trudged into the city of his enemies.
For three days he mumbled God's message under his breath,
hoping no one would hear.

"In 40 days, Nineveh will be destroyed."
No mention of repentance.
No mention of grace.
Simply a much-deserved destruction of the people he despised.

So, after three days, Jonah dusted the dirt from his sandals.
Shortchanged God's call for repentance.
Nineveh had 37 more days to repent,
37 more days to hear the message,
but as far as Jonah was concerned,
if they didn't hear the first time,
"Shame on them."

To the possibilities of forgiveness for the despised Assyrians,
Jonah turned a cold heart.
Clinging to past atrocities of the people of Nineveh,
Jonah climbed to the top of the hill overlooking the great city,
privately praying for fire and brimstone.
Absolute annihilation.

Yet, deep in the marrow of his bones,
he knew God's grace was sufficient.
"Slow to anger, abounding in love and faithfulness."
This was the God Jonah knew.
If Nineveh heard,
Nineveh would respond.

In sackcloth and ashes,
Nineveh repented.
God relented.
Jonah resented.

Counting God's grace to Nineveh as evil,
the prophet's anger burned.
Jonah, the world's worst missionary,
needed a lesson in priorities.

A fast-growing gourd for shade.
Jonah rejoiced.
A hungry worm and a withered plant.
Jonah raged.

God reminded him.
People are more valuable than gourds.
God, the Almighty,
offers mercy and forgiveness
to *all* people who repent and turn to Him.
To think otherwise is human hubris.

Compassion

The contrast between
Jonah's all-consuming anger and God's all-encompassing love
is vividly illustrated in Jonah's story.
Human Capriciousness
versus
Divine Compassion.

God desires relationship with all people,
but Jonah detested the Assyrians.
His prejudice colored his judgment.
God's call to Nineveh ran counter to
every emotion in his heart.
He could not bring himself to obey.

How like Jonah we are!
God calls us to do something
dwelling outside our comfort zone.
We hate the way that feels.
Run in the opposite direction as fast as we can go.

How many storms and raging seas would we avoid if we just
did what God wanted us to do
the first time He called?
How much heartache do we suffer needlessly
because we defy God's will for our lives?

To make matters worse,

sin is so incredibly convenient.

If we want to run from God,

we can always find a boat waiting at the dock,

ready to take us wherever we think our Father cannot find us.

We climb aboard a seductive sailing ship to sin,

headed 180 degrees from where the

Father wants us to go.

We go to Tarshish.

Our rebellion.

Our choice.

Our will.

In the midst of our disobedience

and the storms that ensue,

we find God to be a God of second chances.

A God of compassion.

No matter how far we run,

how big a mess we make of our own lives,

God continually calls us back.

Jonah found a spiritual second chance in the form of a big fish

sent by the loving Father to a prodigal son.

We find second chances around every corner.

God never gives up on us.

Not when we're evil.

Not when we run away.

Not when we shake our fists at him.

Not when we mope on the top of a hill

waiting for God to judge the sinners around us.

Jonah is the anti-hero of his own story.

He is, however, fully human.

He ran.

He argued.

He bargained.

He whined.

He fumed.

He developed a convenient truth...

The men, women and children of Nineveh should die.

They are Assyrians.

No other reason is needed.

Like Jonah,

we quickly condemn the evil in the world.

Rapidly relegate the sinner to the trash heap.

If they don't look or act like us,

we react even slower to be the personal agent of

God's forgiveness.

Basking in the glow of the salvation offered to us.

Balking at sharing that same grace to others.

In a perfect example of our humanity,
Jonah causes us to hang our heads.
We are so like him!
In perfect example of His deity,
God causes us to lift our heads.
He gives us chance after chance
to love more as He loves.

So when we hesitate,
He teaches.
Somewhere in our most reluctant hours,
the Creator of the universe quietly plants a gourd,
sharing a lesson in the priority of grace,
desiring that we finally understand
how deep
and broad
and rich
His love can be.

God's character causes Him to act on behalf of Creation.
Compassion for the Ninevites.
Compassion for you and me.
Compassion that compels us to make known
the deepest desire of God's heart.

The Old Testament proclaims.
"Salvation is of the Lord."

The New Testament promises.
"God so loved the world that He gave His only Son
that whosoever believes in Him shall not perish, but have ever-
lasting life."

Go.
Tell.
Your Nineveh waits.

When he saw the crowds, he had compassion on them,
because they were harassed and helpless,
like sheep without a shepherd.
—Matthew 9:36

FINAL THOUGHT

Without a doubt,
the innocence of the Bible stories learned as a child
took root in a fertile heart.
The gentle encouragement of parents and friends
convinced me of the truth of these simple messages.
Because of these stories and others,
I placed my personal trust in Jesus Christ.

As I grew older,
innocence shattered by the world's tempting influences,
I struggled in my unworthiness.
What is my life compared to these
men and women I placed on a pedestal?

God revealed His answer in sharpest clarity…
like the fresh smell of rain on sun-baked soil.
God adores the flawed,
yet faithful,
who flail around in futility,
until they embrace God's perfect plan for their lives…
at this moment…
in this place…
at this time.

There comes a point when we must put away childish things.
Abandon the spiritual pabulum of convenient faith,
biting deeply into the meat of biblical truth.

To see these Bible characters as perfect examples of
Christian faith is to see them through the eyes of a child.
Their strength lies not in their perfection,
but in their willingness to recognize their personal failings,
seek forgiveness and
find a renewed sense of purpose.
Trusting in the Lord, their God, to direct their feet.
Not just in a moment of inspiration,
but every day they lived.

ABOUT THE AUTHOR

Kirk Lewis, currently serves as Superintendent of the Pasadena (TX) Independent School District. Lewis earned his bachelor's degree in 1976 in advertising/public relations from Texas Tech University where he was named Distinguished Alumnus in 2011. He earned a master's degree in Education Futures from the University of Houston in 1983 and a doctorate degree in Educational Leadership from Lamar University in 2008.

He worked in public relations at the university level and in the corporate world before joining Pasadena ISD in 1986, leading the district's Communication's Department. In 2000, Lewis was named Deputy Superintendent for Administration in Pasadena ISD before becoming Superintendent in 2006.

He served as a youth minister in Wolfforth, Texas, while in college and attended Southwestern Baptist Theological Seminary in 1976-77. He and his wife Robin have been members of South Main Baptist Church in Pasadena, Texas, since 1977. He is a layman, a deacon and has taught adult Sunday School for more than 35 years.

Kirk and Robin's family include two married sons, Adam and Andrew. Adam and his wife Jordan have two children--Eli, almost three-years-old and Josiah, who is seven months old. Andrew and Melissa were married in 2013. All are active members of South Main Baptist Church.